CW01508894

AirPods I

2ND GENERATION

User Guide

The Complete Step By Step Tutorial For Beginners And Seniors To Set Up And Master The Use Of Apple AirPods Pro & AirPods Max With Tips And Trick

BY

RON OSCAR

Copyright © 2023 Ron Oscar

All rights reserved. No part of this book shall be reproduced, stored in a retrieval system, or transmitted by any means, electronic, mechanical, photocopying, recording, or otherwise, without written permission from the publisher. Although every precaution has been taken in the preparation of this book, the publisher and author assume no responsibility for errors or omissions. Nor is any liability assumed for damages resulting from the use of the information contained herein.

TABLE OF CONTENTS

CHAPTER ONE

INTRODUCTION

THE 2022 AIRPODS PRO DESIGN

With the AirPods undergoing a redesign in 2021, it was anticipated that the AirPods Pro would undergo a similar transformation so that the distinctions between the two types of AirPods would become more apparent. However, this has not occurred: the Pro headphones retain their stem and appear identical to the previous variants.

There are a few external differences between this generation and the previous one.

SWIPE BUTTONS

There is one noteworthy external modification. A new touch control sensor located on the stem of the AirPods Pro enables volume control by swiping up or down. This is in addition to the existing touch controls for play, pause, etc.

This is less spectacular than the gesture-based settings predicted by some optimistic analysts based on Apple's filing for a patent in 2020, but it's still a welcome enhancement.

AIRPODS PRO 2022 ENHANCEMENTS

The exterior design has remained essentially identical, while the interior has received significant updates. Here are the essential characteristics you must understand.

BETTER BATTERY LIFE

While we're on the subject of electricity, it's important to note that the recently released AirPods Pro have a significantly longer lifespan of batteries than their previous generations. They have a rating for 6 hours of playing time, which is 33% longer than the first-generation AirPods Pro, and 30 hours with the case included.

CHARGEABLE CONTAINER

The charging case has been upgraded in several enticing ways.

In addition to MagSafe charging devices and Qi-compatible wireless devices, the Apple Watch can now be charged using an Apple Watch puck. This is very convenient for Apple aficionados who are far from home or simply want to declutter their nightstands.

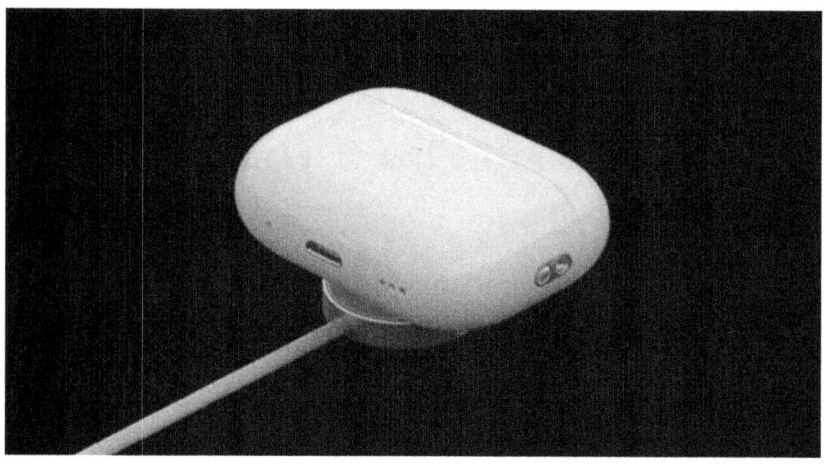

Do you own an Apple Watch? Then, you can charge your AirPods Pro 2022. Also, note the lanyard attachment on the right.

The enclosure now also contains a tiny speaker. This serves two primary purposes: to play location audio for Find My (assisted by a new U1 chip's compatibility with the AirTag's Precision Finding feature) and to audibly signify when the battery's charge is low or charging has begun. In this regard, it complements the visual function of the LED indicator.

The transition from USB-A to USB-C has not yet been implemented into the charging enclosure. It still derives from Lightning. However, it is equipped with a small fastener for attachment to a lanyard or purse.

ENHANCED NOISE CANCELLATION

Apple now includes four sizes of ear tips as opposed to three, and a new extra-small tip has been added to improve passive noise isolation.

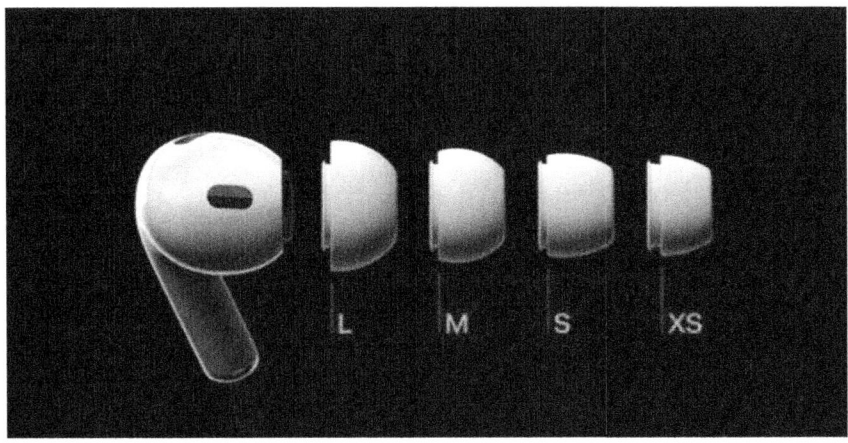

The XS ear tip is a novel option for individuals with small shell-likes

Apple claims that active noise suppression is twice as effective as it was on the previous model, which is a far greater enhancement. This is a result of the new H2 chip's advanced computation and enhanced acoustic algorithms.

Apple is working to reduce pollution even when Transparency Mode is activated, which is intended to let you listen to external audio. The newly introduced Adaptive Transparency feature responds to extremely intense sounds and reduces their volume.

IMPROVEMENT IN AUDIO QUALITY

Perhaps more than anything else, the audio quality of the latest generation of AirPods Pro has been significantly enhanced. Using an innovative feature termed Personalized Spatial Audio and the TrueDepth camera on a suitable iPhone to generate a precise representation of your cranium, the sound can be tailored to the geometry of your ears.

AIRPODS PRO SETUP

HOW TO PAIR AIRPODS

AirPods Pro is compatible with Apple devices for listening to audio, movies, communications, and more. After pairing your AirPods Pro with one Apple device (such as your iPhone), your AirPods will automatically attach to all other Apple devices on which you are registered with the same Apple ID.

AirPods Pro 2nd generation

ACTIVATE LISTENING WITH A PRESS OR A TAP

You can suspend and restore video playback, switch audio tracks, and more with a tap or hold, all without lifting another device.

An interface for playback within the Music app. The Siri icon is active at the bottom of the screen, indicating that Siri is being used to fulfill a request.

EMPLOY SIRI

Siri can be used with AirPods and other Apple devices to discover information, play music, accept or decline incoming calls, and announce app notifications, among other tasks.

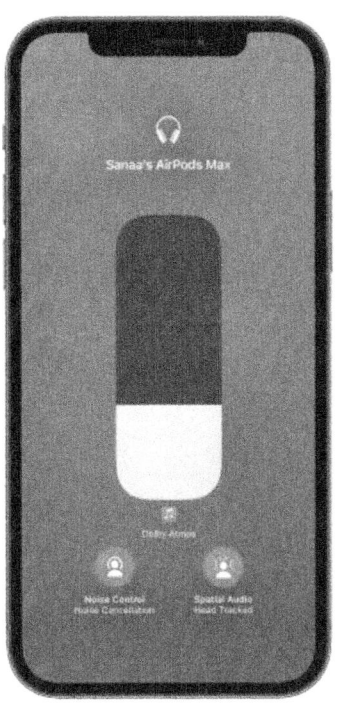

The volume interface in Control Center displaying the AirPods Max volume level. The Noise Control/Noise Cancellation emblem is displayed to the left of the volume indicator, indicating that Noise Control is enabled. The Spatial Audio/Head Tracked icon on the right indicates that Spatial Audio and head tracking are enabled.

IGNORE YOUR SURROUNDING NOISE

Give your complete attention to your beloved song, television program, or podcast. Simply activate Noise Cancellation when donning AirPods Pro (all iterations) or AirPods Max to block out ambient noise. Switch to Transparency mode when you want to hear the canine howl or the kettle whistle.

An interface from the iPhone program Find My. On a map of San Francisco, the location of AirPods is marked with an address and the options Play Sound and Find.

AIRPODS (3RD GENERATION) AND AIRPODS PRO (ALL GENERATIONS) PROVIDE THE OPTIMAL ALIGNMENT

Utilize the Ear Tip Fit Test with AirPods Pro (all iterations) to determine the ear tips that fit you best.

AIRPODS (3RD GENERATION)

A diagram depicting the implantation of AirPods (3rd generation) into the ear.

Press the AirPods gently into your earphones and rotate them toward your face. The fit of your AirPods should be close.

USING THE AIRPODS PRO EARTIP FIT TEST

Run the fit detection test on your iPad, iPod touch, or iPhone to determine which of the included ear tips provides the greatest seal.

Displaying the Ear Tip Fit Test for AirPods Pro (1st generation) on the iPhone's screen.

Open the case for the AirPods Pro, then navigate to the Settings app on your iPad, iPod touch, or iPhone. Touch the label of your AirPods Pro closest to the screen's top, press Ear Tip Fit Test, and then follow the on-screen instructions.

CONTROLS ON AIRPODS

Aside from controlling audio from the applications you use with your AirPods, you can also use the controls on your AirPods to suspend and resume playback, switch tracks, answer conversations, and activate Siri. On your device, you can alter the settings for AirPods (all generations), AirPods Pro (all generations), and AirPods Max.

Go to Settings on your device, then select the label of your AirPods next to the screen's top.

AIRPODS PRO 1st GEN CONTROLS

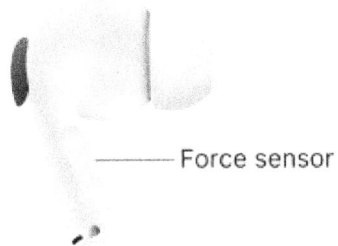

Force sensor

The exact position of the force sensor along the leading edge of each of your AirPods Pro (1st generation).

You may accomplish any of the following with the force detector on the stem of the AirPods Pro (1st generation):

- Pause and play audio: Squeeze the stem. To continue playing, press it again.
- To play the next track, tap the stem twice.
- Play the preceding song: The stem should be pressed three times.
- Accept a call: When a call arrives, squeeze the stem.

- You can configure either of your AirPods to switch between Noise Cancellation mode and Transparency mode when you hold down on the stem.
- You can configure either of your AirPods to activate Siri when the stem is pressed and held.

AIRPODS PRO 2ND GEN CONTROLS

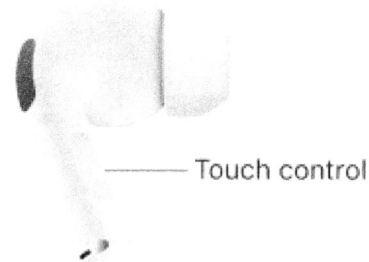

———— Touch control

The exact spot of the Touch function on AirPods Pro (2nd generation), located along the stem of each AirPods.

You can do any of the following with the Touch interface on the base of both AirPods Pro (2nd generation):

❖ Pause and play audio: Squeeze the stem. To continue playing, press it again.
❖ To play the next track, tap the stem twice.
❖ Play the preceding song: The stem should be pressed three times.

- ❖ Accept a call: When a call arrives, squeeze the stem.
- ❖ To adjust the volume, lightly drag the stem up or down.
- ❖ You can configure any one of your AirPods to switch between Noise Cancellation mode and Transparency mode when you hold down on the stem.
- ❖ You can configure any one of your AirPods in order to activate Siri when the stem is pressed and held.

HOW TO PAIR AIRPODS WITH AN APPLE DEVICE

AirPods can be paired with Apple devices in order to listen to audio recordings, video communications, and more. With compatible devices, you may additionally utilize your AirPods to make and receive calls via phone and FaceTime calls.

After pairing your AirPods with a single Apple gadget (such as your iPhone), your AirPods will automatically attach to all other Apple devices on which you are registered with the same Apple ID.

AIRPODS ARE COMPATIBLE WITH IPAD, IPOD TOUCH, AND IPHONE–PAIRING METHODS

Ensure that your device has the most recent version of either iOS or iPadOS running before you begin.

- Go to Settings > Bluetooth on your device, enable Bluetooth, and then perform one of the actions that follow:
  - ✓ AirPods across all generations or AirPods Pro across all generations: Open the case containing your AirPods and place it close to your device.
  - ✓ AirPods Max: Remove the AirPods Max from the Smart Case and, within 60 seconds, position them next to the desired device till the configuration animation displays.

    If the animation does not appear, you can manually associate AirPods Max with your device. Select your AirPods by going to Settings > Bluetooth. Press and hold the volume control button on the AirPods Max for approximately five seconds, or until a white flashing light appears.

- Follow the instructions on-screen, then tap Done.

Ensure your Apple Watch possesses the most recent release of watchOS loaded before proceeding.

❖ Launch the Settings app on Apple Watch, then select Bluetooth.

❖ To connect your AirPods, tap the Bluetooth interface.

If you are attempting to pair AirPods Max but your device is not listed, press and hold the volume control button for approximately five seconds, till the light illuminates white.

Before beginning, ensure that the most recent version of macOS is installed on your Mac.

- On your Mac, navigate to Apple > System Preferences > Bluetooth in the sidebar. Ensure Bluetooth is turned on, and then perform one of the actions that follow:
  ✓ AirPods across all generations or AirPods Pro across all generations: Hold down the setup button on the rear of the AirPods case for

approximately five seconds at a time, or until the status indicator begins to flicker white.

✓ Hold down the volume control switch for approximately five seconds, till the status light illuminates white.

- Select your AirPods from the list of devices, then click Connect.

Tip: You may also display the Bluetooth options in the menu section to make pairing your AirPods simpler.

PAIRING WITH APPLE TV

Ensure your Apple TV has the most recent version of tvOS installed before proceeding.

❖ Select Settings on Apple TV by pressing the TV Control Center icon on the Siri Remote.

❖ Pick Remotes and Devices > Bluetooth, then take one of the following actions:

✓ AirPods across all generations or AirPods Pro across all generations: Hold down the setup button on the rear of the AirPods case for approximately five seconds, or until the status indicator illuminates white.

✓ AirPods Max: Hold down the volume control button for approximately five seconds, till a white flashing light appears.

❖ Under Other Devices, choose your AirPods.

CONNECTING THE AUDIO CABLE TO AIRPODS MAX

Connect a USB Lightning to 3.5 mm Audio Cable from Apple to the port for charging on your AirPods Max and the headphone socket on your device.

AIRPODS CAN BE PAIRED WITH NON-APPLE DEVICES

AirPods are compatible as Bluetooth earpiece with non-Apple devices. You cannot utilize Siri, but you can speak and listen.

Follow these steps to pair your AirPods via a smartphone running Android or an additional non-Apple device:

• Ensure that Bluetooth is enabled on your non-Apple device (on an Android device, navigate to Settings > Connections > Bluetooth).

• Perform one of the subsequent:

- ✓ AirPods across all generations or AirPods Pro across all generations: Unlock the lid, then hold down the configuration button on the rear of the AirPods charging case for approximately five seconds, or until the status light illuminates white.
- ✓ Hold down the button on the volume control switch for approximately five seconds, till the status light illuminates white.
- Select your AirPods when they show up in your list of Bluetooth devices.

UNPAIRING, RESTARTING, OR RESETTING AIRPODS

If your AirPods are not functioning properly, ensure that the device they are paired with is up-to-date. Then, attempt to unpair, restore, or recalibrate them.

UNPAIRING AIRPODS

❖ **Unpair AirPods from your iPad, iPod touch, or iPhone**: select the title of your AirPods close to the very top of the Settings display, then select Forget This Device. This eliminates the AirPods from every device where the same Apple ID is signed in.

❖ **Unpair AirPods from your Apple Watch:** On Apple Watch, navigate to Settings > Bluetooth, tap the Actions Available icon, and then press Forget Device to erase the AirPods from every gadget where the same Apple ID is signed in.

❖ **Unpair AirPods from your Mac:** On a Mac, select Apple > System Settings, select the AirPods' name in the sidebar (and you might have to scroll), and then pick Forget this Device.

❖ **Unpair AirPods from your Apple TV** On Apple Television: Select your AirPods in Settings > Remotes and Devices > Bluetooth. Choose Forget about this Device.

Note: To use your AirPods again after detaching them, you need to connect them with a gadget linked to your Apple ID.

RESTARTING AIRPODS

When your AirPods are not functioning properly, reactivate them.

Perform one of the subsequent:

- AirPods across all generations or AirPods Pro across all generations: Place the AirPods in the case and close the lid for at least ten seconds.

- AirPods Max: On the right earpiece, simultaneously hold down the Digital Crown and the volume control button until the status indicator after the charging port illuminates amber (approximately 10 seconds), and then release the buttons.

Note: when you hold the controls for more than 10 seconds, the AirPods Max will reset to their factory settings.

RESTORE AIRPODS TO THEIR ORIGINAL SETTINGS

When your AirPods are not functioning properly after a restart, you can reset them to factory settings.

Perform one of the subsequent:

❖ AirPods across all generations or AirPods Pro across all generations: Wait 30 seconds after placing the AirPods in their case and closing the lid. Unlock the lid, then hold down the button for setup on the rear of the case for approximately fifteen seconds, till the indicator light alternates between amber and white bursts.

❖ AirPods Max: Regarding the right headphone, simultaneously tap and hold the Digital Crown and the volume control button till the indicator light following the charging connector changes to blinking white (approximately 15 seconds).

CHAPTER TWO

CHARGING YOUR AIRPODS

AIRPODS (ALL GENERATIONS) AND AIRPODS PRO (ALL GENERATIONS) CAN BE CHARGED.

HOW TO CHARGE AIRPODS OR AIRPODS PRO

❖ Place the AirPods in the case.

❖ Close the cover.

AirPods automatically turn off and charge when the case's lid is closed.

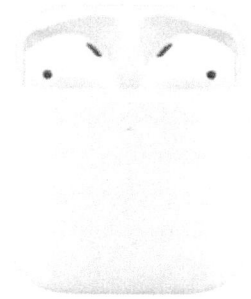

First- and second-generation AirPods in their charging container

The third-generation AirPods in their recharge container.

The first-generation AirPods Pro in their recharge container.

The second-generation AirPods Pro in their charging container.

AIRPODS OR AIRPODS PRO CONTAINER CHARGING

For charging the AirPods or AirPods Pro case, you can either:

- Connect the case to a power receptacle using a Lightning to USB Cable and a power adapter that is compatible with the case.
- AirPods Pro (all generations) should place the charging container with the status indicator facing up in the center of a MagSafe wireless charger or a Qi-certified adapter. • AirPods (2nd iteration) or AirPods (3rd generation) should use a Bluetooth-enabled charging case.

  If you've got AirPods Pro (2nd generation), you can put the case with the status light facing up in the center of an Apple Watch wireless charger.

When the case is appropriately aligned with the charger, the charging status light illuminates for a few seconds before turning off as the container keeps on holding the charge. The charging case for AirPods Pro (2nd generation) plays a tone by default, but you can disable it.

When your AirPods are in their case and the cover is open, the illumination on the case indicates the status of their charge. When your AirPods are not in the case, the light indicates the case's status.

Green indicates a full charge, while amber indicates that less than one complete charge remains. If there is no indicator light, you might have to recharge your AirPods before using them again.

Additionally, you can monitor the battery level of your AirPods on your iPhone, iPad, iPod touch, or Mac.

❖ iPad, iPhone, or iPod touch: Uncover the case's cover with the AirPods inside and hold it near your device. Pause a few a moment to view your AirPods' charge status.

When your AirPods are connected to your device, you can also navigate to Settings and select the AirPods' name near the screen's top to view the charge status.

❖ Mac: Unlock the case lid or remove the AirPods from the case, then connect them to your Mac.

Select the Bluetooth button in the options bar on your Mac, then select your AirPods.

AIRPODS MAX CHARGING

HOW TO CHARGE AIRPODS MAX

Use a Lightning to USB Cable and an appropriate power adapter to link the AirPods Max to a power receptacle.

A cable for powering the AirPods Max.

Note: When you are not using AirPods Max, place them in sleep mode by positioning them in the

Smart Case to conserve battery life. (AirPods Max cannot play audio when they are in the Smart Case.)

CHECK THE STATUS OF CHARGES

On your iPad, iPhone, Mac, or iPod touch, you can verify the charge status of your AirPods Max.

- **iPad, iPod touch, or iPhone**: Wear or hold your AirPods next to your device to ensure that they are connected. Wait a few seconds for the charge status to display.

  If your AirPods have been linked to your device, you may also navigate to Settings and select the AirPods' name near the screen's top to view the charge status.

- **Mac**: Wear or bring your AirPods near your Mac to ensure they are connected. Select the Bluetooth button in the menu bar on your Mac, then select your AirPods.

HOW TO RENAME AIRPODS

You can rename your AirPods with an iPhone, iPad, iPod touch, or Mac. When multiple devices are logged in using the same Apple ID, the new moniker is updated across all devices.

❖ Wear your AirPods and connect them to your iOS device.

❖ Perform one of the subsequent:

  ✓ On Apple's iPad, iPod touch, and iPhone: Touch the label of your AirPods close to the upper part of the screen after navigating to Settings. Tap the existing name, enter the new name, and then tap Done.

  ✓ Choose Apple > System Settings on your Mac, select the label of your AirPods in the bar by the side (you may need to scroll), and then input a new moniker.

CHAPTER THREE

PLAYING AUDIO ON FIRST- OR SECOND-GENERATION AIRPODS

You can double-tap while donning AirPods (1st or 2nd generation) to play, pause, or resume audio on your Mac, iPod touch, iPhone, Apple TV, Apple Watch, or iPad.

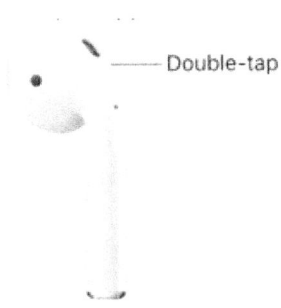

The double-tap location on AirPods (1st and 2nd generation), at the tip of the stem.

PLAYING AND PAUSING AUDIO PLAYBACK

❖ Utilize one or both AirPods and ensure that they are paired with your device.

❖ Open an audio application, then play a file. For instance, you can listen to a song in Apple Music or a book with audio in the Books app.

Remove one AirPod to halt audio whilst hearing with both AirPods. When the device is returned to the ear, playback automatically resumes.

You can also configure one of your AirPods to halt when double-tapped and resume when double-tapped again.

Switch off automated ear detection to prevent AirPods from automatically playing and stopping audio.

HOW TO STOP THE AUDIO

Detach the two AirPods from your earbuds, or if you are only wearing one, remove that AirPod.

HOW TO SKIP TRACKS

In many audio applications, you can double-click to switch to another track. You can double-tap, for example, to move to the adjacent music in Apple Music or earlier episodes in the Podcasts app.

AirPods are displayed. One of the AirPods is double-tapped.

- AirPods (first generation): You can configure double-tapping to continue forward or backward.
- AirPods (2nd generation): When you double-tap, your AirPods will seamlessly transition to the next track.

GUARD YOUR SENSE OF HEARING

Utilizing your iPad, iPod touch, or iPhone, you can track and restrict the volume of your AirPods.

PLAYING AUDIO ON THIRD-GENERATION AIRPODS

Your third-generation AirPods' force sensor may be used to start, stop, or restart audio on your Mac, iPod touch, iPhone, Apple TV, Apple Watch, or iPad.

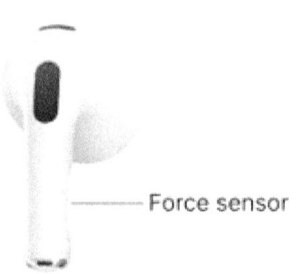

Force sensor

The exact position of a force detector on the base of each of your AirPods (3rd generation).

PLAYING AND PAUSING AUDIO PLAYBACK

❖ Utilize one or both AirPods and ensure that they are paired with your device.

❖ Open an audio application, then play a file. For instance, you can listen to a song in Apple Music or a book that's audio in the Books app.

Remove one AirPod to halt audio whilst listening with both AirPods. When the device is returned to the ear, playback automatically resumes.

If you do not want AirPods to autonomously play and pause audio, you may alter how AirPods terminate a call.

HOW TO STOP THE AUDIO

Detach the two AirPods from your earbuds, or if you are only wearing one, remove that AirPod.

HOW TO SKIP TRACKS

In many audio applications, you can switch to another track by double-pressing the indentation on the stem of either AirPod. For instance, you can press twice the stem's indentation to move to the following song in Apple Music or an earlier episode in the Podcasts app.

To advance to the previous track, triple-press the stem's indentation.

AUDIO PLAYING ON AIRPODS PRO OF ALL GENERATIONS

When donning AirPods Pro (all generations), you can play, pause, or resume audio on your Mac, iPod touch, iPhone, Apple TV, Apple Watch, or iPad, by pressing the indentation on the stem. You can also modify the volume on AirPods Pro (2nd generation) using the Touch control.

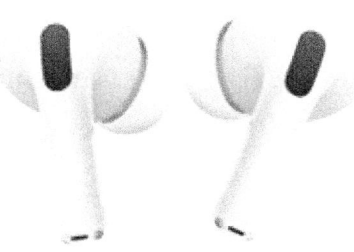

PLAYING AND PAUSING AUDIO PLAYBACK

- Wear one or both AirPods and ensure that they are paired with your device.

- Open an audio application, then play a file. For instance, you can listen to a song in Apple Music or a book that's audio in the Books app.

Remove one AirPod to halt audio while hearing with both AirPods. When the device is returned to the ear, playback automatically resumes.

Note: You can also halt audio by pressing the indent on the stem. Repress the button to resume playback.

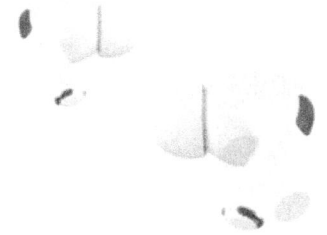

AirPods Pro (first iteration) are demonstrated. The stem of one of the AirPods is being compressed on both sides.

STOPPING THE AUDIO

Detach the two AirPods Pro from your earbuds, or if you are only wearing one, remove that AirPod.

SKIPPING A TRACK

You can double-press the indentation on the stem of either AirPods Pro to move to the next track in a variety of audio applications, like the next track in Apple Music or earlier episodes in the Podcasts app.

To advance to the previous track, triple-press the stem's indentation.

VOLUME CONTROL FOR AIRPODS PRO (2ND GENERATION)

Using the Touch control, you can modify the volume by gently swiping either upward or downward on the indentation on the stem.

You can disable volume control by sliding on the stem if you do not wish to use it.

CHAPTER FOUR

AUDIO PLAYBACK ON AIRPODS MAX

You can play, pause, or bypass audio on your Mac, iPod touch, iPhone, Apple TV, Apple Watch, or iPad while donning AirPods Max.

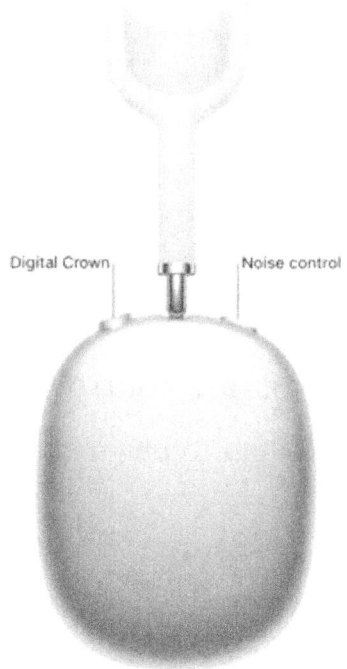

The placement of the Digital Crown and the volume control switch on the right AirPods Max headphone.

PLAYING AND PAUSING AUDIO PLAYBACK

❖ Wear your AirPods and connect them to your iOS device.

❖ The Digital Crown can be pressed to play or halt audio.

STOPPING THE AUDIO

Take your AirPods Max off your cranium (head).

SKIPPING A TRACK

Double-tap the Digital Crown rapidly to continue forward. Quickly click three times upon the Digital Crown to advance backward.

MANAGEMENT OF SPATIAL SOUND AND HEAD MONITORING

When you watch a supported show or movie, make a FaceTime call, or listen to supported music on your device, AirPods (3rd generation), AirPods Pro (all generations), and AirPods Max use spatial sound reinforcement and head monitoring to generate a theater-like environment with a sound that encompasses you.

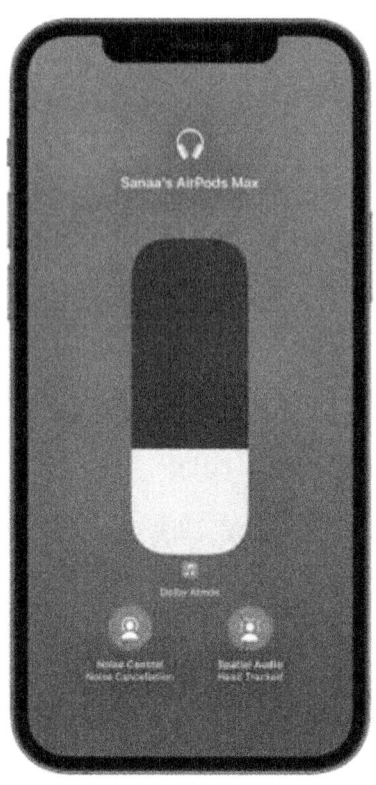

The volume interface in Control Center displaying the AirPods Max volume level. The Sound Control/Noise Cancellation emblem is displayed to the left of the volume indicator, indicating that Noise Control is enabled. The Spatial Audio/Head Tracked icon on the right indicates that spatial sound and head tracking are enabled.

DISCOVER HOW SPATIAL AUDIO OPERATES

When connecting AirPods (3rd iteration), AirPods Pro (all iterations), or AirPods Max to an iPad or iPhone, you can learn more about Spatial Audio.

- Wear your AirPods and connect them to your iOS device.

- Go to Settings on your iPhone or iPad, then select the title of your AirPods close to the very top of the screen.

- Tap Spatial Audio.

UTILIZE CUSTOM SPATIAL AUDIO

You may use an iPhone X or later to produce a picture of your ear and skull form for Personalized Spatial Audio. Your Spatial music setup personalizes music to better match how you perceive sound and synchronizes across all of your Apple devices with the same Apple ID that is running macOS Ventura, iPadOS 16.1, iOS 16, tvOS 16, or later.

To make use of Personalized Spatial Audio, you must either:

❖ Open the case closure with the AirPods inside, place the case near the iPhone, and then follow the on-screen instructions.

❖ Go to Settings on your iPhone, then select the AirPods icon near the highest point of the screen.

Select Personalize Spatial Audio followed by Personalize Spatial Audio.

STOPPING THE USE OF PERSONALIZED SPATIAL AUDIO

Perform any of the options below to discontinue using Customized spatial sound on all of your devices:

➢ iPhone versus iPad Select the label of your AirPods nearer the very top of the screen after navigating to Settings. select Stop Using Personalized Spatial Audio, and then choose Personalized Spatial Audio.

➢ Mac: Select Apple > System Settings, click the AirPods' name in the sidebar, and then select Stop Using Personalized Spatial Audio.

➢ Apple TV: hold down the Siri Remote's TV Control Center button, then select AirPods and Personalized Spatial Audio.

You can configure Personalized Spatial Audio on your iPhone in order to use it again.

CONTROL HEAD TRACKING AND SPATIAL AUDIO ON AN IPAD OR IPHONE

Control Center allows you to manage Spatial Audio and motion tracking for each compatible app.

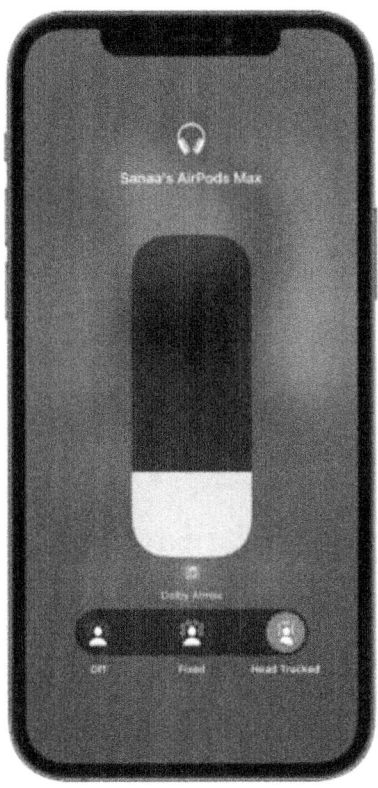

The volume interface in Control Center displaying the AirPods Max volume level. beneath the volume signal are the Spatial Audio settings. There are three choices: Off, Fixed, and Head Tracked.

❖ Wear your AirPods and connect them to your iOS device.

❖ Launch Control Center, contact and press the volume slider, and then select Spatial Audio in the lower right corner.

❖ Select one from the list below:

✓ Head Tracked: Turns both spatial sound and motion detection on. The audio you are listening to will appear to originate from your iPhone or computer.

✓ Fixed: Spatial Audio is now enabled without head tracking.

✓ Off: Both of them Spatial Audio and gaze tracking are disabled.

The settings you select are automatically applied the next time you use the app. For instance, if you select Fixed as you listen to a song in the Music app, the Fixed setting will be applied automatically the next time you play a song from that app.

Note: To turn off head tracking for all applications on an iPhone or iPad, navigate to Settings > Accessibility > AirPods, touch the name of your AirPods, and then disable Follow [device].

MAC USERS CAN MANAGE SPATIAL AUDIO AND MOTION TRACKING

On Mac computers with Apple silicon and macOS 12.2 or later, you can use Spatial Audio and head tracking to make supported television programs, videos, and music sound as if they are emanating from all around you. You can enable or disable spatial sound and motion tracking for each compatible app.

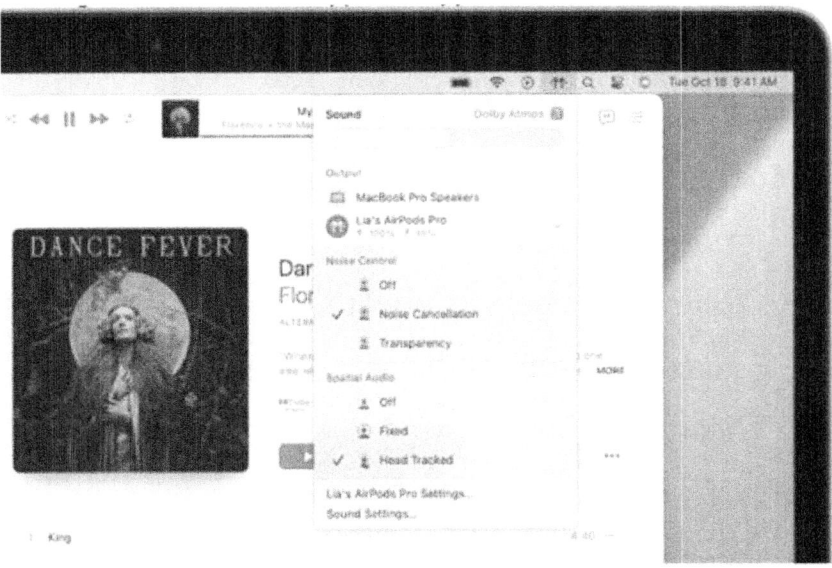

A MacBook Pro display with the Music application playing a song. The AirPods icon is selected in the menu bar, and a menu displays AirPods with sound cancellation and motion-tracked Spatial Audio enabled.

Keep in mind that Spatial audio is not supported by all applications or content.

❖ Make sure that your AirPods have been linked to your Mac.

❖ Select the AirPods symbol in the navigation bar.

When the AirPods symbol is not visible in the menu bar, select Apple > System Preferences > Control Center in the sidebar. Click the menu that appears to the right of Sound, then select constantly display in Menu Bar. (It may be necessary to navigate down.)

❖ Select one of the subsequent Spatial Audio options:

   ✓ Head Tracked: Turns both Spatial Audio and motion tracking on. This enables your ears to follow your head's movement.

   ✓ Fixed: Spatial Audio is now enabled without head tracking.

   ✓ Off: Both Spatial Audio and gaze tracking are disabled.

USING APPLE TV 4K TO CONTROL SPATIAL AUDIO AND THE HEAD MONITORING

Employing Control Center on Apple TV 4K, you can personalize the Spatial Audio parameters for each supported application. You can also enable or disable head monitoring for all applications. (Requires tvOS 15.1 or later.)

- Make sure that your AirPods have been linked to the Apple Television 4K.
- To enable or disable Spatial Audio, launch Control Center, pick your AirPods, and then select Spatial Audio.

The settings you select are automatically applied every subsequent time you use the application. For instance, if you activate Spatial Audio while employing the Apple TV application with the TV Control Center icon on your AirPods, Spatial Audio will be activated immediately the next time you use that application with your AirPods.

Note: To turn off dynamic head tracking for all Apple TV 4K applications, double-click the TV Control Center icon ⬚ on the Siri Remote, navigate to Settings ◉ > Accessibility > AirPods, and then disable Center Audio on the TV.

CHAPTER FIVE

AUDIO SHARING USING BEATS HEADPHONES AND AIRPODS FROM COMPATIBLE IPAD, IPHONE, AND IPOD TOUCH

You may discuss what you're enjoying with a friend wearing suitable AirPods or Beats while wearing AirPods. Both pairs of headphones must be coupled with an iPad, iPod touch, or iPhone that is compatible.

WHEN AN ACQUAINTANCE WEARS AIRPODS OR BEATS HEADPHONES, YOU CAN SHARE AUDIO

If your companion has suitable AirPods or Beats headsets, you may share the audio from your device with them (supported models only).

❖ Wear your AirPods and connect them to your iOS device.

❖ Touch the Playback Destination icon on your device's Currently Playing screen, Lock Screen, or Control Center.

❖ Select Share Audio (below your headphones' moniker).

❖ Bring the headphones of your companion near the iPod touch, iPhone, or iPad.

❖ Tap Audio Sharing on your device.

❖ Request that your companion select **Join on their device**.

MODIFY THE VOLUME AND POLLUTION CONTROL SETTINGS

If you and a companion share audio from your device using compatible AirPods or Beats headphones, you can select a separate volume level for each pair of headphones. Additionally, for AirPods Pro as well as AirPods Max, you may choose a distinct audio control setting for each user.

• Open Control Center on your device, then contact and press the volume control.

• Drag the sound sliders to adjust the volume level.

• To alter the noise management mode (AirPods Pro or AirPods Max), touch one of the Volume Control controls at the bottom of the display, then select an option.

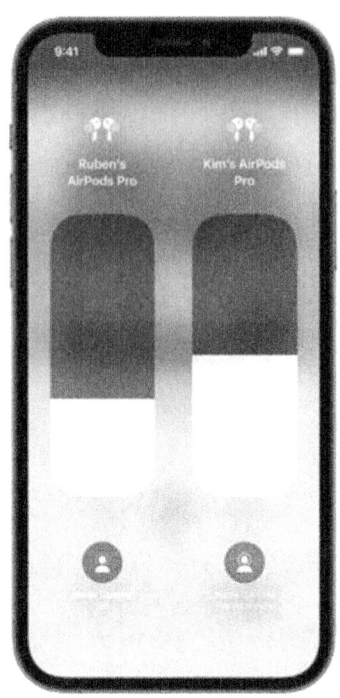

The volume display in Control Center displays the volume levels for two pairs of AirPods. The Noise Control/Transparency emblem is displayed to the left of the volume indicator, showing that Transparency is enabled. The Noise Management/Noise Cancellation emblem is displayed to the right of the audio indicator, indicating that Noise Control is enabled.

DISCONTINUE SHARING OF AUDIO

➤ Select the Playback Destination icon on your device's Currently Playing screen, Lock Screen, or Control Center.

➤ To disconnect from your friend's headphones, tap their name.

APPLE TV 4K ALLOWS AIRPODS AND HEADPHONES MADE BY BEATS TO SHARE AUDIO

Apple TV 4K can transmit music to a maximum of two pairs of Apple headphones that are wireless, like the AirPods or Beats headphones, to reduce background noise.

Note: When sharing audio with several headphones, Spatial Audio, and head tracking cannot be used. Apple TV HD does not support sharing audio.

- To open Control Center, hold down the TV icon on the Siri Remote.

- Select the Destination for Playback icon .

- Click on Headphones, and then choose the desired headphones.

- Click Share Audio, and subsequently follow the instructions displayed on-screen to connect the second set of headphones.

AIRPODS CAN BE SWITCHED BETWEEN APPLE DEVICES

When you're signed in with the same Apple ID on all of your Apple devices, your AirPods (on supported AirPods) connect seamlessly to whichever device you're listening to.

For instance, if you're enjoying audio on your computer with AirPods and your iPhone begins playing a podcast, song, or other audio, your AirPods will automatically transition to the iPhone. Your AirPods automatically transition to the iPhone when you receive a call.

SWITCHING AIRPODS TO YOUR APPLE IPAD, IPHONE, OR IPOD TOUCH

❖ Select the Playback Destination icon on the Currently Playing screen, Lock Screen, or Control Center.

❖ Select a pair of AirPods.

STOP AIRPODS FROM CONNECTING TO YOUR IPHONE, THE IPAD, OR THE IPOD TOUCH

If your AirPods transfer to another device while you enjoy listening to music on your iPod touch, iPhone, or iPad, you can simply swap them back.

In the "Moved to" notice at the top of the screen, press the Return Headphone Connection icon.

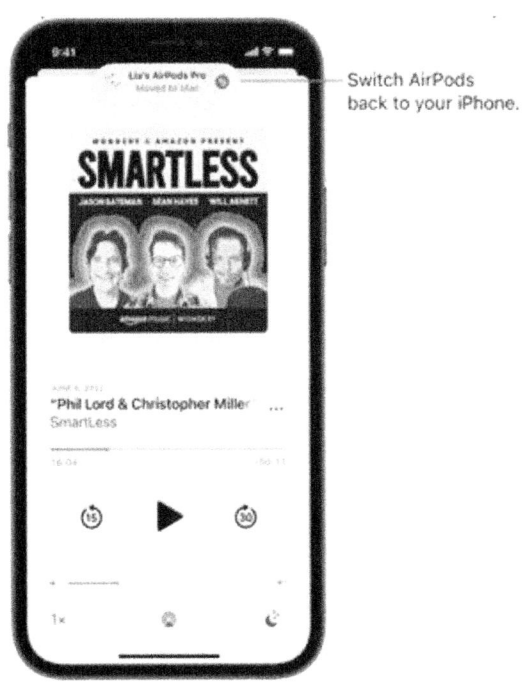

The iPhone Lock Screen with the message "AirPods Pro Moved to iPad" and a toggle to move the AirPods back to the iPhone.

Follow these steps if you aren't interested in your AirPods to transition automatically:

- Wear your AirPods and connect them to your iOS device.
- Go to Settings on your iPod touch, iPhone, or iPad, then select the name of the AirPods that you have near the screen's top.
- Touch Connect to This Device, and then tap Last Time This Device Was Connected.

REPLACE AIRPODS WITH AN APPLE WATCH

If your AirPods have been connected to an Apple Watch, you can quickly transition from another device to your Apple Watch to listen to audio.

➢ Wear your AirPods near your Apple Watch.
➢ Tap the audio you wish to listen to on your Apple Watch, such as a song in Apple Music or an episode in Apple Podcasts.
➢ To connect, tap the name of your AirPods.

REPLACE AIRPODS WITH MAC

Perform one of the subsequent:

❖ Select your AirPods by clicking the Bluetooth icon in the menu bar and then selecting them.

❖ Select Apple menu > System Settings, choose Sound in the sidebar, select Output on the right, and finally pick your AirPods.

STOP AIRPODS FROM CONNECTING TO YOUR MAC

Do the following if you do not want your AirPods to connect automatically to your Mac:

➢ Wear your AirPods and connect them to your iOS device.

➢ Select Apple > System Settings on your Mac, then select the name of your AirPods in the sidebar.

➢ Select "When this Mac was last connected" beneath Connect to This Mac.

On occasion, a notification regarding your AirPods appears on the display of your Mac. Click the Connect icon to affirm that you want to pair your AirPods with your Mac or another device.

REPLACE AIRPODS WITH APPLE TV

If your AirPods are paired with your Apple TV, you can effortlessly transition from another device to your Apple TV to listen to audio.

❖ Put on your AirPods close to your Apple TV.

❖ Press the TV Control Center button on the Siri remote once the name of your AirPods appears on Apple TV.

SET UP SIRI

When AirPods are paired with an iPhone, iPad, iPod touch, Apple Watch, or Mac, Siri can be used to access information, play audio, accept or decline inbound phone calls and FaceTime calls, and more.

CONFIGURE UP SIRI ON THE GADGET

If you haven't activated "Hey Siri" on your iPod touch, iPhone, iPad, Apple Watch, or Mac, you can do one of the following:

- Apple's iPad, iPod touch, and iPhone: Navigate to Settings > Siri & Search and enable Listen for "Hey Siri."

- The Apple Watch Navigate to Settings > Siri and enable Listen for "Hey Siri."

- Mac: Select Apple > System Settings, select Siri & Spotlight in the sidebar, toggle Ask Siri on the right, and then toggle "Listen for 'Hey Siri'." (It may be necessary to navigate down.)

SIRI IS CAPABLE OF SETTING UP ANNOUNCE CALLS

You can enable Siri to notify you of incoming calls when using compatible headphones. Perform one of the subsequent:

❖ Apple's iPad, iPod touch, and iPhone: Select Always, Headphones & Car, or Headphones Only by navigating to Settings > Siri & Search > Announce Calls.

❖ AirPods: Wear them with your Apple Watch. Go to Settings > Announce Notifications on your Apple Watch, then enable Announce Notifications.

MANAGE WHICH NOTIFICATIONS ARE DISPLAYED

When you're wearing AirPods and they're linked using your iPhone, iPad, iPod touch, or Apple Watch, time-sensitive notifications are audibly announced automatically. You can select which applications as well as how regularly you receive notifications.

• On Apple's iPad, iPod touch, and iPhone: Navigate to Settings > Notifications, then select the desired app. Scroll down and tap the Announce Notifications button.

- On the Apple Watch, Navigate to Settings > Siri > Announce Notifications menu. Scroll up, and then select the applications for which you'd like to get audio notifications.

You can restrict alerts when you require focus. See Focus Configuration in the iPhone User Guide.

MODIFY THE PREFERENCES TO TURN ON SIRI WITH A SINGLE TAP

The controls on your AirPods can be used to activate Siri. Configure either AirPods (2nd generation) to turn on Siri with a double tap, or configure either AirPods Pro (1st generation) to engage Siri when the force sensor is pressed and held.

- ❖ Wear your AirPods and connect them to your iOS device.
- ❖ Navigate to Settings on your device, then select the title of your AirPods at the very top of the display.
- ❖ Click Left or Right followed by Siri.

Note: By default, the buttons on AirPods (1st and 3rd generation), AirPods Pro (2nd generation), and AirPods Max are set to activate Siri.

CHAPTER SIX

AIRPODS MAX CAN MAKE AND RECEIVE CALLS

MAKING AND RECEIVING CALLS

- AirPods Max should be worn and linked to the iPod touch, iPhone, iPad, or Apple Watch (cellular or Wi-Fi).

- Perform one of the subsequent:
  - ✓ On an iPad or iPhone (Wi-Fi + Cell model), say "Hey Siri" followed by "Call Eliza's mobile" to make a call. On an iPad with no cellular, utter something like "Make a FaceTime call," or hold down the Digital Crown, pause for a chime and then make the request you want to make.
  - ✓ To accept or terminate a contact, hit the Digital Crown.

Note: If you enable announce phone calls, you may additionally utilize your voice to receive or decline a call.

The position of the Digital Crown on the opposite side of the AirPods Max earbud

Note that you may change the volume by turning the Digital Crown while a call is going on.

REJECT AN INCOMING CONTACT

When AirPods Max is paired with an iPhone, you can reject incoming calls and dispatch them directly to voicemail.

When an incoming call is received, double-tap the Digital Crown.

AIRPODS MAX CAN HANDLE A SECOND CALL

❖ Select the Digital Crown to place the first call wait and handle the second call when a second call arrives.

❖ Perform any of the subsequent:
  ✓ Tap the Digital Crown to toggle between conversations.
  ✓ Click twice the Digital Crown to terminate the active contact and transfer to the one that is on hold.

AIRPODS ALLOW USERS TO LISTEN TO AND REPLY TO COMMUNICATIONS

Make use of your AirPods (second or third generation), AirPods Max, or AirPods Pro (all iterations), to listen to iPad, iPod touch, or iPhone messages. When the gadget has been locked, the AirPods you're using are connected, and a notification arrives, a chime will ring and Siri will be able to relay the message to you.

ACTIVATE ANNOUNCE MESSAGES

If you did not enable Announce Messages when you initially activated your AirPods (2nd or 3rd gen), the

AirPods Pro (all gens), or AirPods Max, you can enable them at any time.

Navigate to Settings > Notifications > Messages on your device, then enable Announce Notifications.

You can also select the types of notifications you wish to receive.

Note: Before you can enable Announce Messages, you must enable Announce Notifications in Settings > Notifications.

RESPOND TO MESSAGES

After Siri has read a message, say "Reply that's great news."

The communication is repeated, and affirmation is required before it is sent.

RESPOND WITHOUT AWAITING VERIFICATION

For applications that allow you to submit a reply, such as the Messages app, Siri echoes what you said before requesting affirmation before transmitting your reply.

For sending replies without conformation, use any of the following methods:

❖ On Apple's iPad, iPod touch, and iPhone: Turn on Reply Without Confirmation by navigating to Settings > Notifications > Announce Notifications and activating Reply Without Confirmation.

❖ Go to Settings > Siri > Announce Notifications on your Apple Watch, then enable Reply Without Confirmation.

STOP HAVING SIRI READ YOU A MESSAGE

You may choose from the following options:

➢ The second-generation AirPods: Say "Stop" or "Cancel," or double-tap on either AirPod.

➢ Press the force sensor on AirPods (3rd gen) and AirPods Pro (1st gen).

➢ Press the Touch button on your AirPods Pro (2nd generation).

➢ AirPods Max: Use the Digital Crown button.

CHAPTER SEVEN

ADJUST AIRPODS (1ST AND 2ND GEN) PARAMETERS

AirPods (1st and 2nd gen) settings can be modified on an iPad, iPhone, iPod touch, or Mac. You can customize the action conducted as you tap twice on your AirPods, disable automated ear identification, and much more.

First- and second-generation AirPods

CHANGE THE FUNCTION OF THE DOUBLE STROKE

You can alter the double-tap action conducted by your AirPods.

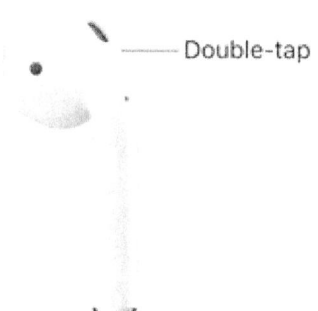

Double-tap

❖ **The double-tap location on AirPods (1st and 2nd gen), at the tip of the stem**

❖ Wear your AirPods and connect them to your iOS device.

❖ Perform one of the subsequent:

  ✓ On Apple's iPad, iPod touch, and iPhone: Select the label of your AirPods close to the highest part of the screen after navigating to Settings.

  ✓ On a Mac, select Apple > System Settings, then pick the AirPods name in the sidebar (you might have to scroll).

❖ Select Left or Right, and then select the action you wish to be performed whenever you double-click on one of your AirPods.

CONFIGURE THE MICROPHONE PLACEMENT FOR YOUR AIRPODS

- Wear your AirPods and connect them to your iOS device.
- Perform one of the subsequent:
  - ✓ On Apple's iPad, iPod touch, and iPhone: Touch the title of your AirPods close to the very top of the display after navigating to Settings.
  - ✓ On a Mac, select Apple > System Settings, then pick the AirPods name in the sidebar (you may need to scroll).
- Choose the Microphone, then one of the subsequent options:
  - ✓ Automatically Switch AirPods: You can use either AirPod as a microphone. If only one is used, it functions as the microphone.
  - ✓ Always Right or Always Left: whichever direction you select becomes the microphone, regardless of whether it is in your ear or its case.

DISABLE AUTOMATED AUDITORY DETECTION

Your AirPods automatically pause audio playback when you remove them and resume when you replace them. You can alter this configuration.

- Wear your AirPods and connect them to your iOS device.
- Perform one of the subsequent:
  - ✓ On Apple's iPad, iPod touch, and iPhone: Tap the AirPods' name near the top of the Settings screen, then toggle Automatic Ear Detection either off or on
  - ✓ On Mac, select Apple > System Settings, touch the AirPods name in the sidebar (you might need to navigate), and toggle "Automatic ear detection" on or off.

Additionally, you can adjust the audio level of the sounds produced by your AirPods.

CHANGE PARAMETERS FOR AIRPODS (3RD GEN)

On the iPad, iPhone, iPod touch, and Mac, AirPods (third generation) settings can be modified. For instance, you can set the location of the microphone and disable automatic auditory detection.

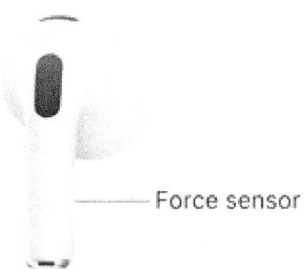

Force sensor

The exact position of the force detector on the base on every one of your AirPods (3rd generation)

CONFIGURE THE MICROPHONE PLACEMENT FOR YOUR AIRPODS

❖ Wear your AirPods and connect them to your iOS device.

❖ Perform one of the subsequent:

✓ On Apple's iPad, iPod touch, and iPhone: Tap the label of your AirPods close to the very top of the display after navigating to Settings.

✓ On a Mac, select Apple > System Settings, then pick the AirPods name in the sidebar (you might have to scroll).

❖ Choose the Microphone, then one of the subsequent options:

✓ Automatically Switch AirPods: You can use either AirPod as a microphone. If only one is used, it functions as the microphone.

✓ Always Right or Always Left: whichever direction you select becomes the microphone, regardless of whether it is in your ear or its case.

CHANGE HOW TO END A CALL USING AIRPODS

Typically, you can terminate a call with one press of the base on your AirPods, but you have the option to use two presses instead.

➢ Wear your AirPods and connect them to your iOS device.

➢ Perform one of the subsequent:

✓ On Apple's iPad, iPod touch, and iPhone: Touch the label of your AirPods close to the very top of the display after navigating to Settings. Tap the End Call button, then select Press Once or Press Twice.

✓ On a Mac, select Apple > System Settings, then pick the AirPods name in the sidebar (since you might have to scroll). Select an option to the right of "End call."

DISABLE AUTOMATED AUDITORY DETECTION

Your AirPods automatically pause audio playback when you remove them and resume when you replace them. You can alter this configuration.

- Wear your AirPods and connect them to your iOS device.
- Perform one of the subsequent:
  - ✓ On Apple's iPad, iPod touch, and iPhone: Tap the AirPods' name near the top of the Settings screen, then toggle Automatic Ear Detection either off or on.
  - ✓ On Mac, select Apple > System Settings, click the AirPods name in the sidebar (since you might have to navigate), and toggle "Automatic ear detection" on or off.

ADJUST AIRPODS PRO (ALL MODELS) PARAMETERS

On an iPod touch, iPhone, Mac, or iPad, you may modify the AirPods Pro settings. You can personalize the action conducted when pressing and holding the force sensor on AirPods Pro (1st iteration) or Touch control on AirPods Pro (2nd version), alter the location of your microphone, disable the automated ear sensor, and more.

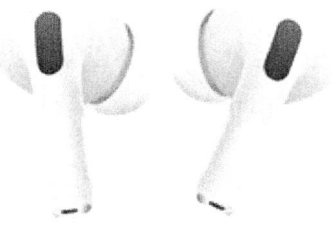

AirPods Pro (second-gen)

CHANGE THE BEHAVIOR OF THE FORCE DETECTOR OR TOUCH CONTROL

You can modify the action executed when you tap and retain the indentation on the AirPods Pro stem.

❖ Wear your AirPods and connect them to your iOS device.

❖ Perform one of the subsequent:

- ✓ On Apple's iPad, iPod touch, and iPhone: Select the label of your AirPods close to the very top of the display after navigating to Settings.
- ✓ On a Mac, select Apple > System Settings, then pick the AirPods name in the sidebar (and you might have to scroll).
- ❖ Select Left or Right, and then select the action you wish to be performed whenever you touch and hold the stem indentation.

CHANGE HOW TO END A CALL USING AIRPODS

By standard, you can terminate a call with one press of the stalk on your AirPods, but you may elect to use two presses instead.

- ➢ Wear your AirPods and connect them to your iOS device.
- ➢ Perform one of the subsequent:
  - ✓ On Apple's iPad, iPod touch, and iPhone: Touch the label of your AirPods close to the very top of the display after navigating to Settings. Tap the End Call button, then select Press Twice or Press Once.

✓ On a Mac, select Apple > System Settings, and then select the AirPods name in the sidebar (and you might need to scroll). Select an option to the right of "End call."

CONFIGURE THE MICROPHONE PLACEMENT FOR YOUR AIRPODS

- Wear your AirPods and connect them to your iOS device.

- Perform one of the subsequent:

  ✓ On Apple's iPad, iPod touch, and iPhone: Touch the label of your AirPods close to the very top of the display after navigating to Settings.

  ✓ On a Mac, select Apple > System Settings, then pick the AirPods name in the sidebar (and you might have to scroll).

- Choose the Microphone, then one of the subsequent options:

  ✓ Automatically Switch AirPods: You can use either AirPod as a microphone. If only one is used, it functions as the microphone.

  ✓ constantly Left or Always Right: whichever direction you select becomes the microphone, regardless of whether it is in your ear or its case.

DISABLE AUTOMATED AUDITORY DETECTION

The AirPods Pro automatically pause audio playback when you remove them and recommence when you replace them. You can alter this configuration.

❖ Wear your AirPods and connect them to your iOS device.

❖ Perform one of the subsequent:

   ✓ On Apple's iPad, iPod touch, and iPhone: Tap the AirPods' name near the top of the Settings screen, then toggle Automatic Ear Detection either off or on.

   ✓ On Mac, select Apple > System Settings, click the AirPods name in the toolbar (you may need to navigate), and toggle "Automatic ear detection" on or off.

TURNING OFF CHARGING CASE SOUNDS FOR AIRPODS PRO (SECOND GEN)

Your AirPods Pro (2nd gen) charging case emits sounds when it pairs, charges, and performs other functions. You may disable these noises.

- Wear your AirPods and connect them to your iOS device.
- Perform one of the subsequent:
  - ✓ On Apple's iPad, iPod touch, and iPhone: Select the label of your AirPods close to the very top of the Settings screen, then toggle Allow Charging Case Sounds either off or on.
  - ✓ On a Mac, select Apple > System Settings, hit the label of your AirPods in the sidebar (and you might have to navigate), and toggle "Enable charging case sounds" on or off.

CHAPTER EIGHT

MODIFY AUDIO CONFIGURATIONS FOR AIRPODS MAX

On the iPad, iPhone, iPod touch, and Mac, AirPods Max settings can be modified. For instance, you can alter the behavior of the Digital Crown and the volume control button, disable automated head identification, and more.

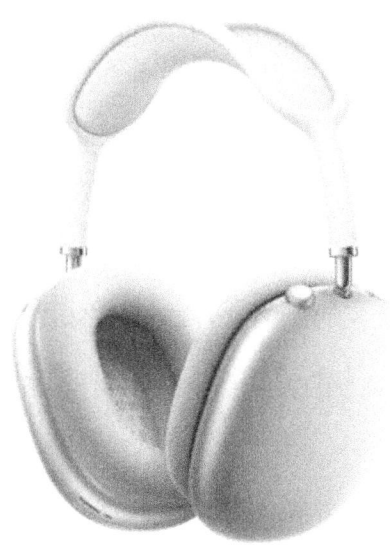

AirPods Plus

CHANGE THE OPERATION OF THE DIGITAL CROWN

Change the direction in which you rotate the Digital Crown to adjust the sound level on AirPods Max.

The position of the Digital Crown on the right AirPods Max earbud

➢ Wear your AirPods and connect them to your iOS device.

➢ Perform one of the subsequent:

✓ On Apple's iPad, iPod touch, and iPhone: Touch the label of your AirPods close to the very top of the display after navigating to Settings. Select Digital Crown, followed by a selection.

✓ On a Mac, select Apple > System Preferences, then pick the AirPods Max name in the sidebar (and you might need to scroll). Select an option to the right of "Increase volume by rotating the Digital Crown."

MODIFY THE VOLUME CONTROL SWITCH

Pressing the noise reduction button on the right AirPods Max headphone toggles between Transparency mode and Active Noise Cancellation mode.

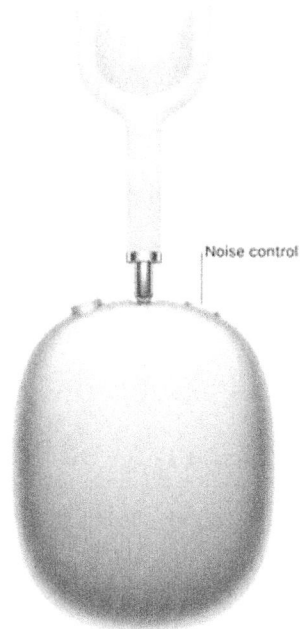

The position of the noise-controlling switch on the right AirPods Max earbud.

❖ Wear your AirPods and connect them to your iOS device.

❖ Perform one of the subsequent:

✓ On Apple's iPad, iPod touch, and iPhone: Touch the label of your AirPods close to the very top of the display after navigating to Settings. Select the desired modes by pressing the volume control icon. When you press the volume control button on AirPods Max while listening to the audio on your device, it cycles using all of the choices you selected on your device.

✓ On a Mac, select Apple > System Preferences, then pick the AirPods Max name in the sidebar (and you might be required to scroll). On the right, choose an option next to "Press button to cycle between." When you press the volume control option on AirPods Max while listening to the audio on your Mac, it cycles via all of the choices you picked on your Mac.

DEACTIVATE AUTOMATIC HEAD DETECTION

Your AirPods Max instantly pauses audio playback when you remove them and recommence when you replace them. You can alter this configuration.

- Wear your AirPods and connect them to your iOS device.
- Perform one of the subsequent:
  - ✓ On Apple's iPad, iPod touch, and iPhone: Tap the AirPods' name near the top of the Settings screen, then toggle Automatic Head Detection either off or on.
  - ✓ On a Mac, select Apple > System Settings, click the AirPods' name within the left (you might need to navigate), and toggle "Automatic head detection" on or off.

SWITCHING BETWEEN MODES OF TRANSPARENCY AND NOISE CANCELLATION

While listening to the audio on all generations of AirPods Pro or AirPods Max, you can alternate between Transparency and Noise Cancellation modes. Noise Cancellation eliminates extraneous noise, while Transparency mode lets you hear the outside world. You can also use AirPods Pro (2nd generation)'s Adaptive Transparency feature to automatically reduce noisy noises around you.

ADJUST THE TRANSPARENCY AND NOISE CANCELLATION SETTINGS ON YOUR AIRPODS

Perform one of the subsequent:

❖ Wear your AirPods Pro and hold down the indentation on the stem of one of your AirPods until you hear a chime.

AirPods Pro displayed. One AirPod is being compressed on the stem

• AirPods Max: Put on your AirPods Max and select the noise-canceling switch on the right earbud. The modification is confirmed by a chime.

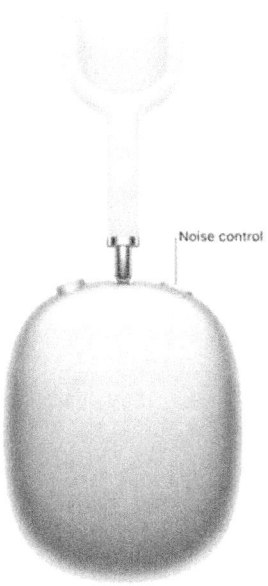

Noise control

The position of the volume control switch on the right AirPods Max earbud's tip.

CONTROL THE TRANSPARENCY AND NOISE CANCELLATION SETTINGS ON YOUR IPAD, IPOD TOUCH, OR IPHONE

❖ Utilize one or both AirPods and ensure that they are paired with your device.

❖ Hold down the volume button while Control Center is open.

❖ Select the Noise Control icon in the bottom left corner, then select one of the options below.

  ✓ **Noise Cancellation**: Eliminates external noises.

- ✓ **Off**: Deactivates Transparency and Noise Cancellation modes.
- ✓ **Transparency**: Allows you to hear ambient sounds.

The volume interface in Control Center displaying the AirPods Max volume level. Noise suppression options are displayed beneath the volume indicator. The options are Noise Cancellation, Off, and Transparency, from left to right.

When using the Transparency mode on AirPods Pro (all iterations), you can also customize which sounds are heard.

APPLE WATCH TRANSPARENCY AND NOISE CANCELLATION SETTINGS

- Utilize one or both AirPods and ensure that they are paired with your Apple Watch.

- Tap the AirPlay icon while listening to the audio, and then select a volume control mode.

MAC TRANSPARENCY AND NOISE CANCELLATION SETTINGS

❖ Employ one or both AirPods and ensure that they are paired with your Mac.

❖ Perform one of the subsequent:

  ✓ Select a noise cancellation mode by clicking the AirPods Pro or AirPods Max symbol in the menu bar.

  ✓ Select Apple menu > System Settings, click the AirPods' name in the sidebar (you may need to navigate), and then choose a noise reduction option on the right.

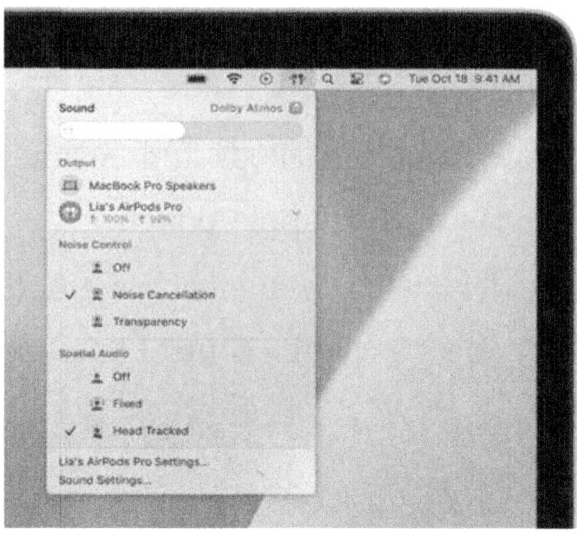

On a Mac, the AirPods symbol is chosen in the menu bar's upper-right corner. Noise Cancellation is chosen below Noise Control and Head Tracking is selected below Spatial Audio for AirPods Pro (all generations).

ADJUST APPLE TV'S TRANSPARENCY AND NOISE CANCELLATION SETTINGS

- Put on one or both AirPods and connect them to your Apple TV.

- Select the AirPods icon in Control Center, and then alter the controls.

PERMIT NOISE CANCELLING IN ONE EAR

Utilize your AirPods Pro, and perform one of these things:

❖ On Apple's iPad, iPod touch, and iPhone: Tap AirPods in the Settings > Accessibility > AirPods menu. Noise Cancellation can be activated with One AirPod.

❖ Tap the name of your AirPods in Settings > Accessibility > AirPods, then activate Noise Cancellation with One AirPod.

❖ Choose Apple > System Settings on the Mac, then select Accessibility in the sidebar and Audio on the right (you may need to scroll). Click the Info icon adjacent to your AirPods, and then activate Noise Cancellation with One AirPod.

❖ Navigate to Settings > Accessibility > AirPods on your Apple TV, then activate Noise Cancellation using just one of your AirPods.

UTILIZE ADAPTIVE TRANSPARENCY WITH THE SECOND-GENERATION AIRPODS PRO

You can switch on Adaptive Transparency on AirPods Pro (2nd gen) to reduce harsh noises in your environment.

• Wear both AirPods and ensure that they have been linked to your device.

• Go to Settings on your iPhone or iPad, select the label of your AirPods close to the very top of the display, and then enable Adaptive Transparency.

CHAPTER NINE

CONFIGURE HEADPHONE SUPPORT FOR AIRPODS

When using supported AirPods with an iPad, iPod touch, or iPhone, you can adjust the AirPods' accessibility parameters to meet your hearing requirements. Adjust certain frequencies and amplify gentle noises to make music, videos, phone conversations, and recordings sound more distinct and distinct. When you possess an audiogram in the Health application on your iPhone, you can customize your audio using the audiogram.

❖ Navigate to Settings > Accessibility > Audio/Visual > Headphone Accommodations and enable Headphone Accommodations on your iPad, iPod touch, or iPhone.

❖ Tap Custom Audio Configuration and then adhere to the on-screen instructions. Or explicitly configure any of the subsequent:

✓ Select Balanced Tone, Vocal Range, or Brightness for Audio Tuning.

✓ Choose from Slight, Moderate, or Strong gentle sound amplification.

✓ Apply these audio configurations to phone conversations.

✓ Apply these audio configurations to media playback.

✓ Transparency Mode is available on AirPods Pro (all gen): To hear what's going on around you, activate Custom Transparency Mode and modify the amplification, balance, and tone.

❖ To listen to a sample of your audio settings, select Play Sample.

PLAY IDENTICAL AUDIO IN BOTH OF YOUR AIRPODS

When using supported AirPods with an iPhone, iPad, iPod touch, Apple Watch, or Mac, you may utilize Mono Audio instead of stereo sound to play the same content in both earbuds.

Perform any of the subsequent:

• On Apple's iPad, iPod touch, and iPhone: Navigate to Settings > Accessibility > Audio/Video and enable Mono Audio.

• Go to Settings > Accessibility on your Apple Watch, and enable Mono Audio below Hearing.

- On a Mac, select Apple > System Preferences > Accessibility in the sidebar (and you might have to navigate). Click Audio on the right and enable "Play stereo audio as mono."

BACKGROUND NOISES CAN BE PLAYED ON AIRPODS

When using supported AirPods with an iPad, iPod touch, or iPhone, you can play soothing sounds, such as the ocean or rain, to conceal undesirable environmental noise and reduce distractions, allowing you to concentrate or rest.

The Hearing Devices interface within Control Center. It comprises Headphone Level in decibels, Background Sounds, Volume With Media, Live Listen, and Headphone Accommodations, from top to bottom.

- ❖ Wear your AirPods and connect them to your iOS device.
- ❖ Go to Settings > Accessibility > Audio/Visual > Background Sounds on your device, then enable Background Sounds.
- ❖ Configure one of the following:
  - ✓ Choose a sound, and the audio file will be downloaded to your device.
  - ✓ Slide the volume slider.
  - ✓ Adjust the background sound volume when music or other media is playing on your device.

UTILIZE LIVE LISTEN ON AIRPODS

Live Listen is capable of amplifying sound. Position your iPod touch, iPhone, or iPad close to what you wish to hear, then use your AirPods to eavesdrop. This can improve your hearing in certain situations, such as when holding a discussion in an environment that is noisy.

- Wear your AirPods and connect them to your iOS device.

- Launch Control Center on the gadget, touch the Hearing Devices icon , press your AirPods' name, and then hit Live Listen.

If you cannot locate the Hearing Devices icon in Control Center, add it by navigating to Settings > Control Center and selecting Hearing.

- Place your device close to the auditory source.

CUSTOMIZE AIRPODS PRO TRANSPARENCY MODE (ALL GENERATIONS)

When using AirPods Pro in Transparency mode to listen to audio, you will also hear ambient sounds. When using Transparency mode on an iPad, iPod touch, or iPhone, you may modify which audio is transmitted.

REDUCE THE QUANTITY OF BACKGROUND NOISE IN TRANSPARENCY MODE

When your AirPods Pro is connected to an iPad, iPod touch, or iPhone, you can lower the amount of background noise you hear by switching to Transparency mode.

❖ Put on your AirPods and pair them with an iOS smartphone.

❖ On your iPad, iPod touch, or iPhone, go to Settings > Accessibility > Audio/Visual > Headphone Accommodations to confirm that the feature is turned on.

❖ Tap Transparency Mode, select Custom Transparency Mode, and then activate Ambient Noise Reduction.

❖ In Transparency mode, modify the extent to which outside noise is blocked by dragging the slider.

USE CONVERSATION ENHANCERS

You may utilize conversation enhancement if your AirPods Pro is linked to an iPod touch, iPhone, or iPad in order to focus on the individual speaking in front of you. This makes face-to-face conversations simpler to understand.

• Put on your AirPods and pair them with an iOS smartphone.

- On your iPad, iPod touch, or iPhone, go to Settings > Accessibility > Audio/Visual > Headphone Accommodations to confirm that the feature is turned on.
- Tap Transparency Mode, activate Custom Transparency Mode, and then activate Conversation Boost.

CHANGE AIRPODS' FORCE SENSOR, TOUCH CONTROL, AND BUTTON SETTINGS

You can alter the button, force sensor, and Touch control parameters for your AirPods (3rd gen), AirPods Pro (all models), and AirPods Max on your iPod touch, iPhone, iPad, or Apple TV.

ADJUST IPAD, IPOD TOUCH, OR IPHONE FORCE SENSOR, TOUCH CONTROL, AND BUTTON SETTINGS

➢ Navigate to Settings > Accessibility > AirPods on the iPad, iPod touch, or iPhone.
➢ Select a pair of AirPods.
➢ Choose one of the options below:

✓ Push Speed: While an action requires multiple button presses, force sensor presses, or Touch control presses, alter how rapidly you need to press before the action is executed.

✓ Hold down Duration: Adjust the amount of time needed to press and hold the controls, force detector, or Touch control before an action occurs on your AirPods.

✓ Turn off Volume Swipe if you do not want to regulate the intensity by sliding upward or downward on the indentation on the stem of your AirPods Pro (2nd gen).

To access additional options including Headphone Accommodations, select Audio Accessibility Settings.

MODIFY FORCE DETECTOR OR BUTTON CONFIGURATIONS USING A MAC

❖ Choose Apple > System Settings on your Mac, then select Accessibility in the sidebar and Audio on the right side (and you might have to scroll).

❖ Click the Info icon adjacent to your AirPods, and afterward configure any of the options below.

✓ Adjust the rate at which you must strike the controls or force sensor in order to initiate an action that requires multiple presses.

✓ Hold down Duration: Set the amount of time obligated to hold down the controls or force sensor before a reaction occurs.

To access additional options, including Headphone Accommodations, tap Audio Accessibility Settings.

CHANGE APPLE WATCH FORCE DETECTOR, TOUCH CONTROL, AND BUTTON SETTINGS

• Wear your AirPods and ensure that they are paired with your Apple Watch.

• Choose settings by navigating to Settings > Accessibility > AirPods on your Apple Watch.

APPLE TV ALLOWS YOU TO MODIFY FORCE DETECTOR, TOUCH CONTROL, AND BUTTON CONFIGURATIONS

➢ Make sure that your AirPods have been linked to the Apple Television.

➢ Navigate to Settings > Accessibility > AirPods on your Apple TV, then modify any of the following:

- ✓ Press Speed: If an action needs multiple button presses, force sensor presses, or Touch control presses, alter how rapidly you need to press before the action is executed.
- ✓ Hold down Duration: Modify the amount of time needed to hold down the controls, force detector, or Touch control before an action occurs on your AirPods.

ADJUST THE SOUND EFFECT VOLUME FOR AIRPODS

You can change the volume of audio effects performed by your AirPods, like when they are inserted into your earpiece, when you hold down the Touch control in AirPods Pro (2nd gen), or when you receive battery drain alerts.

ADJUST THE SOUND EFFECT AMPLITUDE USING AN IPAD OR IPHONE

- Wear your AirPods and connect them to your iOS device.
- On your iOS device, navigate to Settings > Accessibility > AirPods.

- Choose your AirPods and then modify the Tone Volume.

To access additional options including Headphone Accommodations, select Audio Accessibility Settings.

ADJUST THE SOUND EFFECT VOLUME USING APPLE WATCH

❖ Wear your AirPods and ensure that they are paired with your Apple Watch.

❖ Adjust the Tone Volume by navigating to Settings > Accessibility > AirPods on your Apple Watch.

ADJUST THE SOUND EFFECT VOLUME USING APPLE TV

- Make sure that your AirPods are connected to your Apple TV.

- Go to Settings > Accessibility > AirPods on your Apple TV, select your AirPods, and then modify the Tone Volume.

CHAPTER TEN

FIND AIRPODS USING FIND MY

If you lose your AirPods, you may utilize Find My on your iOS device, iPad, Apple Watch, or Macintosh to locate them. You can also locate your AirPods on iCloud.com/find.

A display of the Find My app on an iPhone. On a map of San Francisco, the location of AirPods Pro is displayed alongside an address and choices for Play Sound, Find, and Notifications.

OVERVIEW OF FIND MY USING AIRPODS

❖ Find My is compatible with all AirPods versions, but certain models may include extra functions to help you locate them.

❖ You must activate Find My on an attached computer (like an iPhone or Macintosh) before losing your AirPods in order to locate them.

❖ Make sure your associated device is running the most recent release of iOS, iPadOS, watchOS, or macOS for the best use of Find My.

❖ You can enable Find My Network to locate certain AirPods models when they are beyond range from the gadget you're using. If the Find My network is disabled (or if your AirPods do not support the Find My network), the Find My app displays the time and location of the last connection.

❖ If the AirPods you're using are beyond the range or require charging, Find My may display their last recorded location, "No location," or "Offline." If they reconnect, you will receive a notification on the devices you connected with them.

VIEW A MAP OF YOUR AIRPODS LOCATION

The Find My app displays the current or past location of your AirPods.

➢ On the iPhone and iPad: Launch the Find My app, select Devices, and then select your AirPods.

➢ Open the Find Devices app on your Apple Watch, and then select your AirPods (needs a Wi-Fi or cell connection).

➢ On a Mac, launch Find My, select Devices, and then pick your AirPods.

➢ On iCloud.com, you can: Login in with your Apple ID at iCloud.com/find, select All Devices, and then pick your AirPods.

If your AirPods are divided on the majority of AirPods models, you only have access to the location one at a time. To find both, locate the one that appears on the map, return it to its case, and then reload the road map to find the other.

If you're using AirPods Pro (2nd iteration), the location of your AirPods and charging case are displayed on a map.

PLAY AN AUDIO TRACK ON YOUR AIRPODS

AirPods can produce a tone to help you find them if they are out of their container. When you're using AirPods Pro (2nd iteration), the charging case may play a sound.

- On an iPhone or iPad, launch the Find My app, select Devices, then tap the AirPods' name, followed by Play Sound.

- Open the Find Devices app on your Apple Watch, select your AirPods, and then tap Play Sound (a Wi-Fi or cell connection is required).

- On a Mac, launch Find My, select Devices, choose your AirPods, tap More Info, and then choose Play Sound.

- On iCloud.com, go to iCloud.com/find, enter your Apple ID, choose All Devices, pick your AirPods, and then click Play Sound.

Your AirPods perform a tone to help you identify them for a few minutes, or until you silence the sound. If your AirPods are not paired with your device and Find My Network is not enabled, the ringtone will play the subsequent time they link to a Wi-Fi or cell phone network.

Tip: When your AirPods are separated, you can disable one of them to make it simpler to locate them individually. click or Tap Right or Left while the sound streams on your AirPods.

LOCATE YOUR AIRPODS IF CLOSE

When your AirPods (3rd gen), AirPods Pro (all versions), or AirPods Max are nearby, such as in a different room of your home, your iPad or iPhone can help you locate them. When you're wearing AirPods Pro (2nd gen), you can locate your AirPods and charging case with pinpoint accuracy.

❖ Launch the Find My app on an iPad or iPhone that was linked with your AirPods in the past.

❖ Tap Devices, then tap the AirPods' name, and then tap Find.

❖ Begin to move around to find your AirPods while adhering to the on-screen instructions.

If you're using AirPods Pro (2nd iteration), you could see a pointed object indicating the correct direction of your AirPods, a distance indicating exactly how far removed they are, and a message if they're on a different floor.

Additionally, you can broadcast a tone on your AirPods to help you locate them. You may have the option to activate the illumination, which may assist you locate your AirPods in low-light conditions.

IDENTIFY AIRPODS AS LOST

If you lose your AirPods (3rd gen), AirPods Pro (1st gen), or AirPods Max, you can mark them as missing and include your contact information in a message.

If you own the AirPods Pro (2nd gen), you can designate each AirPod and the case as lost individually if you lose just one or your AirPods have been detached from the case —iOS 16, iPad operating system, MacOS Ventura, or later required.

- On your device, perform one of the subsequent actions:
  - ✓ Apple's iPad, iPod touch, and iPhone: Open the Find My iPhone app, press Devices, touch

the label of your AirPods, and then tap Activate below Mark as Lost.

- ✓ Apple Watch: Launch the Find Devices app, select a device, select Lost Mode, and then enable Lost Mode.
- ✓ Mac: Launch the Find My app, select AirPods, select the Info icon, and then click Activate.

Follow the instructions on-screen.

ACTIVATE FIND MY NETWORK

When the Find My network is activated, you can view the precise location of AirPods (3rd gen), AirPods Pro (all iterations), and AirPods Max in the Find My app for up to 24 hours after their last connection to your device, even if they are not nearby.

To make use of the Find My network with AirPods Pro (2nd gen), you must have iOS 16, iPadOS 16.1, or macOS Ventura or later.

Essential: Before AirPods are lost, the Find My network has to be active for the Find My app to be able to locate them when they are inactive.

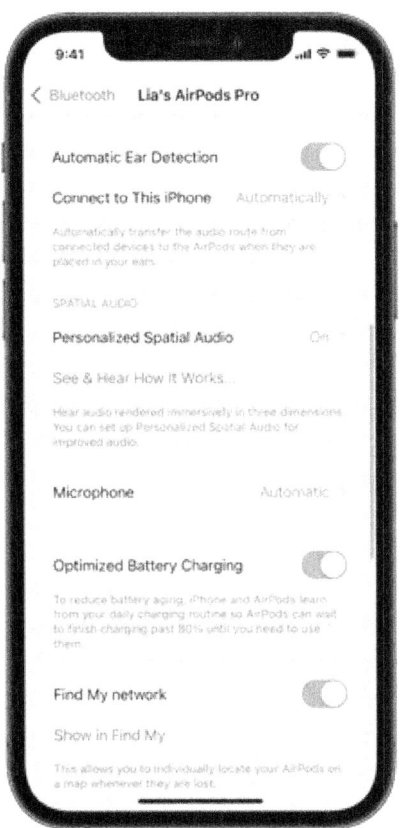

iPhone Bluetooth settings displaying AirPods Pro (all iterations) options. The "Find My Network" option is enabled, allowing missing AirPods to be identified individually on a map.

❖ Wear your AirPods and connect them to your iOS device.

❖ Touch the label of your AirPods close to the very top of the display after navigating to Settings.

❖ Scroll down and activate Find My Network.

Note: If multiple Apple IDs are used with your AirPods (3rd gen), AirPods Pro (all iterations), or

AirPods Max, only the user who activated the Find My network can view them in the Find My app. You may also receive a notification if another person's AirPods have been taken with you.

RECEIVE SEPARATION ALERTS IF YOUR AIRPODS ARE LEFT BEHIND

If the Find My network is active, the Find My app can be used to set alerts to notify you if you've left the AirPods (3rd gen), AirPods Pro (all iterations), or AirPods Max left behind. You can establish trusted locations, such as your residence, and receive alerts on your iPod touch, iPhone, iPad, Mac, or Apple Watch whenever you leave your AirPods somewhere else.

To use the Find My network with AirPods Pro (2nd gen), you'll require iOS 16, iPadOS 16.1, or macOS Ventura or later.

ENABLE SEPARATION NOTIFICATIONS ON YOUR IPAD, IPOD TOUCH, OR IPHONE

- Launch the Find My App, select Devices, and then tap the AirPods' name.

- Select Notify When Left Behind beneath Notifications.
- Enable the Notify When Left Behind option, and then follow the on-screen instructions.
- Select a suggested location or touch New Location, pick an area on the map, and then tap Done to add an authorized location.
- Tap Done.

Note: When you want to be notified of separate notifications, make sure that the Find My application can send you notifications.

ENABLE SEPARATION NOTIFICATIONS ON APPLE WATCH

➢ Launch the Find Devices application on your Apple Watch, and then select the AirPods' name.
➢ Scroll up and tap the Notify When Left Behind button.
➢ Enable Notification When Left Behind.

ENABLE SEPARATION ALERTS ON YOUR MAC

- Launch the Find My Devices app, then tap Devices.

- After selecting your AirPods, click the Actions Available icon.

- Click the Notify When Left Behind link under Notifications.

- Enable the Notify When Left Behind option, and then follow the on-screen instructions.

- To add a trusted location, select a suggested location from the drop-down menu or click New Location, pick an area on the geographical map, and then click Done.

- Click Done.

Printed in Great Britain
by Amazon

59901453R00067